INTRODUCTION

The XFF-1 at Anacostia for Navy trials during the winter of 1931 - 1932. This was the first aircraft in a long dynasty of Grumman naval fighters. *(National Archives)*

Had the Grumman FF project not come to fruition the USN would have, in all probability, missed out on the series of Grumman fighters which included the famous F6F Hellcat of WW2 and finished with the F-14 Tomcat.

A FIGHTER WHICH WAS BORN BY ACCIDENT

In the late 1920s Grumman was known only as a float designer and producer for such USN types as the Loening amphibian. However the Grumman team had been thinking about designing an aircraft for the US Navy although the opportunity had not yet appeared. This eventually came in 1930 when the company became aware of a requirement for a two-seat shipboard fighter, which included a request from the Bureau of Aeronautics (BuAer) to see if the new retractable undercarriage designed by Grumman could be adapted to existing carrier fighters such as the Boeing F4B and Curtiss F8C. Grumman was reluctant to let others benefit from its successful undercarriage design and Roy Grumman, backed by his chief engineer Bill Schewendler, decided to undertake the design of a new fighter for the Navy. This received the factory designation G-5.

This design for a high performance two-seat fighter was submitted in March 1930 and the BuAer immediately expressed a great interest in this proposal.

Because of lack of funds, and also because Grumman was a newcomer in this field, the project did not get underway for a year, when a contract was signed on 28 March 1931 for one prototype with the USN designation of XFF-1 and allocated the BuAer number A8878.

A NEW DINASTY IS BORN

When the XFF-1 made its first flight on 29 December 1931 no one could have imagined that it was the first aircraft of a long dynasty. It was powered by a 575-hp Wright R-1820-E radial driving a two-blade ground-adjustable propeller which gave a top speed of 195 mph, 7 mph faster than the F4B! It also incorporated an enclosed cockpit with dual sliding canopies and a fully retractable main landing gear. The prototype was of all-metal construction, which was relatively new for its time, although the wings were still fabric covered. The armament of the XFF-1 was conventional with two forward firing 0.30-in machine guns complemented by a single machine-gun, on a flexible mount, in the rear cockpit.

The tests, completed at Anacostia, were satisfactory and eventually led to an order, for 27 production aircraft (BuNo 9350-9376), on 19 December 1932 under the designation of FF-1.

After modifications the XFF-1 became the FF-1. It is seen here in flight and shows its landing gear in the extended position. At the beginning of the thirties the USN was looking for new equipment for its aircraft however, in the case of retractable landing gear, the USN was still reluctant to introduce it on its aircraft as it was unsure if it was strong enough to withstand landing on an aircraft carrier. *(National Archives)*

U.S. NAVY

FF-1 8878

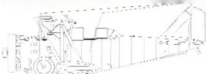

DELIVERIES AND STRENGHT

Month	Delivered	Total delivered	Acc.	Str.	On Hand
February 33	1	1	-	-	1
.../...					
April 33	1	2	-	-	2
May 33	-	2	-	-	2
June 33	7	9	-	-	9
July 33	2	11	-	-	11
August 33	6	17	-	-	17
September 33	6	23	-	-	23
October 33	3	26	-	-	26
November 33	2	28	-	-	28
.../...					
February 35	-	28	1	-	27
.../...					
April 36	-	28	1	-	26
.../...				-	
August 36	-	28	1	-	25
.../....					
March 37	-	28	1	-	24
.../...				-	
July 37	-	28	1	-	23
.../...					
January 38	-	28	1	-	22
.../...					
August 38	-	28	2	-	20
September 38	-	28	2	-	18
October 38	-	28	-	-	18
November 38	-	28	-	1	17
.../...					
May 39	-	28	-	1	16
.../...					
October 39	-	28	-	1	15
.../...					
September 40	-	28	-	1	14
October 40	-	28	-	-	14
November 40	-	28	-	1	13
.../...					
March 41	-	28	-	1	12
April 41	-	28	-	-	12
May 41	-	28	-	1	11
June 41	-	28	-	2	9
.../...					
October 41	-	28	-	1	8
November 41	-	28	-	1	7
December 41	-	28	-	-	7
January 42	-	28	-	2	5
.../...					
April 42	-	28	-	3	2
.../...					
July 42	-	28	2	-	-

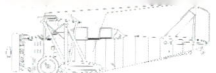

1 XFF-1 ordered against contract 21520 dated 28.03.31.

Officially accepted on 11.02.33

A8878

(c/n 101) NAS Anacostia 29.12.31; Hampton Roads 28.01.32; NAS Anacostia 09.02.32; Grumman for modifications 23.02.32; NAS Anacostia 21.04.32; Grumman 23.05.32; NAS Anacostia 13.06.32; Grumman for modifications (as FF-1) against contract 27654 01.07.32; NAS Anacostia 21.10.32; Norfolk 17.11.32; Grumman 30.11.32; NAS Anacostia 02.12.32; Norfolk 06.12.32; NAS Anacostia 07.12.32; San Diego BatFor 12.01.33; VF-5B 12.01.33; NAS San Diego for repair (date unrecorded, but accident occured on 28.03.33), task completed 14.04.33 and returned to VF-5B; NAS San Diego 20.06.33 for major repair completed 12.01.34; NAS Anacostia 18.01.34; NAF 01.05.34; NAS Anacostia 17.07.34; NAF for OH 04.02.35, completed 03.05.35; NAS Anacostia 08.05.35; ; NAS Norfolk 05.02.36 for repair completed 21.04.36; NAS Anacostia 23.04.36; NAF for construction test 12.05.36; NAS Anacostia 12.06.36. Crashed on 04.03.37 at 1400 at Prince George County (MD):

"The pilot made a forced landing at a point about 8 miles northeast of the station while returning from an authorised flight to Harford (CT). The landing was attempted on a very rough field in an uphill direction. On landing, the landing gear failed and the plane turned over on its back. Inspection showed the gasoline had been exhausted from all tanks. The plane on its flight to Hartford had consumed 86 gallons of gasoline plus an indeterminate amount from the rear twenty-gallon tank. This would indicate a consumption of from 43 to 53 gallons a hour, depending of the amount of gasoline remaining in the rear tank. It is known that for the trip to Hartford and return a total of 226 gallons were consumed, which, after deducting 18 gallons for 3 warming-up periods, shows that the plane consumed 48 gallons per hour for the entire trip. The pilot, on his return flight, stopped at North Beach Airport (NY) after 40 minutes elapsed time and the next day continued on to NAS Anacostia. On both these flights the records of the aerological office of this station indicate that even if the pilot been certain that both the main and auxiliary tank had been filled he could, with 2 warming-up periods, only have hoped to remain in the air for a period of 2 hours and 30 minutes with a 48 gallon fuel consumption. With the adverse wind conditions aloft it is not believed that sufficient allowance was made for a safe completion of the flight."

[LT (jg) C.L.Miller, USN, pilot with 1,844.6 hours flying time including 8.7 of the type, safe]. DBR. **Str.31.03.37**. (TT: 1,501.9 H).

The prototype was later modified as a conventional fighter and became a standard FF-1 whereupon the X was dropped from the designation. *(National Archives)*

Grumman FF-1 BuNo 9350 was the first production aircraft but was never allocated to the VF-5B. It was used at the Naval Aircraft Factory for two years before to be converted to FF-2. *(National Archives)*

TECHNICAL DATA
GRUMMAN FF-1

Manufacturer :
Grumman Aircraft Engineering Corporation
(Bethpage, NY)

Type :
Carrier-based fighter

Accommodation :
Pilot and Observer/rear gunner

Power plant :
One 700 hp Wright R-1820-78

Fuel & Oil
Fuel (US Gal):
120 [454 l]
(two 82 main tanks and one 38 gal reserve tank)

Oil (US Gal) : Standard : 8.5 [32 l]

Dimensions :
Span : 34 ft 6 in [10,52 m]
Length : 24 ft 6 in [7,47 m]
Height : 11 ft 1 in [3,38 m]
Wing area : 310 Sq ft [28,80 m²]

Weights :
Empty : 3,221 lb [1 461 kg]
Gross : 4,800 lb [2 177 kg]

Performance :
Max speed : 207 mph at 5,300 ft
[333 km/h at 1 615 m]
Cruising speed : 180 mph [290 km/h]
Initial climb : 1,600 ft/min [485 m/min]
Service ceiling : 22,400 ft [6 830 m]
Range : 647 miles [1 041 km]

Armament :
2 x fixed forward-firing 0.30-in [7,62 mm] gun
with 500 rpg
1 x dorsal 0.30-in [7,62 mm] gun with 600 rounds

THE UNITS

The first three sections (Red, White and Blue) of VF-5B flying in close formation over the ocean. Although VF-5B was the only unit to be fully equipped with the FF-1 it must be said that VF-1B embarked on the USS *Saratoga*, received two FF-1s, BuNo 9366 for one day, and 9376 pending delivery of its SF-1 which arrived six weeks later. *(National Archives)*

VF-5B

code : 5-F

April 1933 - April 1936

The 27 FF-1s, which were delivered to the USN between April and November 1933, were very similar to the modified XFF-1. Indeed during testing at Anacostia the USN asked for a new engine, a 750-hp Wright R-1820-F (R-1820-78) to be installed as well as a redesigned canopy and changes to minor details. With this new engine its rate of climb became acceptable to the Navy and production aircraft were delivered with the latest modifications incorporated.

The FF-1s only equipped one squadron, VF-5B, which initially embarked on USS *Lexington*. The aircraft, which were soon called "Fifis", replaced this unit's ageing Boeing F4B-2s. VF-5B began to receive its new aircraft in June 1933 and by the end of the month seven aircraft (BuNo 9351-9357) were on its establishment. These were followed by two others (BuNo 9358-9359) in July and four more (BuNo 9360-9362, 9365) in August. However it was not before January 1934

that the full complement of 18 FF-1 was reached. It soon became apparent that some of the pilots had mixed feelings about the FF-1. Criticism was made about the cockpit canopy (indeed many pilots chose to fly with the canopy open!), and the landing gear, which was retracted and extended by hand, received some criticism. The latter was considered troublesome as it gave pilots another job to carry out during landing and take off when maximum concentration was required for other tasks. It must be said that this kind of criticism surfaced when any new equipment was introduced and it was not aimed solely at Grumman's new fighter. Another point of non dissatisfaction was apparent during landing as the FF had a tendency to bounce on touch down and the pilots lacked a good forward view when landing.

Nevertheless the FF served on the USS *Lexington* until the autumn of 1935 when the unit was reassigned to the USS *Ranger*. By November 1935 the VF-5B lost half of its FFs and had received nine F2F-1s as a temporary measure pending the arrival of its F3F-1s. These arrived at

Grumman FF-1 BuNo 9359, VF-5B, USS *Lexington*, 1934. Its regular pilot was Ensign Corliss.

5-F-9

9359

FF-1

U.S. NAVY

Ens's Corliss

the squadron in March and April 1936, and after that date the FF was withdrawn from front line service. During the three years that VF-5B operated the type no FF-1s were lost in accidents which is a very good safety record for a military aircraft of that time.

This did not mean that no FF-1 was lost during those three years and the first FF to be lost, on 2 February 1935, was BuNo 9361. During a ferry flight, with two other FF-1s, to the Naval Aircraft Factory at San Diego Lieutenant (jg) C.W.Pate from the VS-1 got lost in bad weather and was killed, along with Lieutenant (jg) S.G.Sturgess from the VF-3. During another ferry flight BuNo 9360, just after its withdrawal from VF-5B, became the second FF-1 to be lost. The aircraft was being ferried to Philadelphia on 24 April 1936 to be modified to FF-2 configuration when the pilot made too steep a turn during the approach to Santa Monica and crashed, killing both men on board. The operational career of the FF-1 was brief, just three years, however it had been intended from the beginning that the FF was an experiment with the concept of a two-seat fighter, with an enclosed cockpit and retractable undercarriage. The latter two items proved successful but the two seat fighter did not and the USN did not put another two-seat fighter, the Douglas F3D, into service with its carrier squadrons for another fifteen years.

THE MAIN USERS (two and more aircraft assigned)	
VF-1B	2
VF-5B	27
BAD-1	2
NRAB Anacostia (DC)	2
NRAB Glenview (Chicago IL)	7
NRAB Grosse Ile (MI)	5
NRAB Kansas City (KS)	7
NRAB Minneapolis (MN)	2
NRAB Opa Locka (Miami, FL)	4
NRAB Philadelphia (PA)	2
NRAB St Louis (MO)	3

FF-1 BuNo 9363 just before touching down the deck. It was a phase with which the pilots were not very comfortable as the FF-1 had a tendency to bounce on touch down. *(National Archives)*

The last two sections (Green and Yellow) flying in open formation. In front is BuNo 9365 coded 5-F-15. It flew with VF-5B between 29.08.33 and 15.11.34, with this code, before being overhauled and returned to the squadron in April 1935. As in the photo in the previous page, all the pilots are flying the canopy open!
(National Archives)

Just after their conversion to FF-2, BuNos 9372 and 9376 were allocated to NRAB Minneapolis and were respectively the second and third taken on charge by this NRAB, the first being BuNo 9369. The section colours for reserve units were normally the same as fleet units. This seems to be the case here, and consequently BuNo 9376 should be #3 with its lower part of its cowling painted red. *(National Archives)*

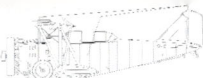

Second line duties

After a short career with the only front line unit to be equipped with the FF-1 the "Fifis" were transferred to Navy Reserve units.

By the spring of 1936, 22 FF-1s were still serving with the US Navy and all surviving aircraft had been converted to FF-2s by the Naval Aircraft Factory in Philadelphia. Intended for use as fighter-trainers, the FF-2s were fitted with dual flight controls and, as they were not intended to be used on aircraft carriers, the tail hook was removed. The forward firing machine-guns were normally retained, however there were exceptions to this. An exhaust collector ring was fitted in place of the individual exhaust stacks used on the FF-1. Finally all the aircraft which had not previously been fitted with radios had these installed.

After conversion to FF-2s the aircraft were distributed amongst the various Naval Reserve Aviation Bases (NRAB), across the country. In some cases the aircraft were pooled when a USN Reserve unit and a USMC Reserve unit were located at the same base. They were used to give refresher courses to reserve pilots or pilots temporarily posted to non-flying duties. Some, at a later time in their career, were used as liaison aircraft for the bases or units.

Despite the accident free operational career of the FF-1 the FF-2's service was a different story. The first accident, to BuNo 9374, occurred on 16 July 1936 and both the pilot and passenger were killed. This happened during the return leg of an authorised cross country flight from Grosse Ile and there were no witnesses to the crash when the aircraft struck the ground at high speed. The next 12 months, until 10 July 1937, were accident free until FF-2 (BuNo 9363) took off from Glenview for a test flight and was wrecked when the pilot went into a flat spin and could not recover in time. The passenger escaped with injuries but the pilot was killed. Six months later, on 8 January 1938, another FF-2 (BuNo 9370) based at NRAB Kansas City was lost during camera gun practice, fortunately without fatalities, but the worst had yet to come. Between 4 August 1938 and 24 September 1938 four FF-2s (BuNos 9351, 9365, 9366, 9372) were lost in training accidents, fortunately with no fatalities. The FF-2 continued to be used to train pilots until the attack on Pearl Harbour, and by December 1941 only 7 aircraft remained in the US Navy inventory as many aircraft never received an authorisation to be overhauled and had been withdrawn from service when this became due. With the outbreak of war, and the increasing availability of more modern trainers, the FF-2s ceased to be of practical use and the final withdrawal of the type was imminent. However before this was implemented another two FF-2s (BuNos 9357 and 9367) were lost, in July 1942. The remaining aircraft were withdrawn from service and the last was struck from the Navy's inventory that same month.

BuNo 9356 warming up for a test flight after its conversion to an FF-2 at the Naval Aircraft Factory. Tactical markings have not yet been applied. *(National Archives)*

27 FF-1s ORDERED (BuNos 9350-9376) AGAINST CONTRACT 27654 DATED 19.12.32.

9350

(c/n 104) Del 25.04.33 Anacostia; NAF 05.06.33; Anacostia 31.07.33; NAF 08.08.33, Norfolk BatFor16.04.35 for OH and **FF-2** conversion completed on 22.09.36; NRAB Kansas 31.07.37. Declared obsolete 18.10.39. **Str.31.10.39** (TT: 550.6)

9351

(c/n 105) Del 08.06.33 Anacostia; San Diego BatFor 21.06.33 for VF-5B; San Diego BatFor 03.01.35 for OH completed 02.04.35; NAF 07.02.35; San Diego BatFor 22.04.35; VF-5B 23.04.35; San Diego BatFor 21.06.35; VF-5B 30.07.35; San Diego BatFor 14.04.36; NAF 08.05.36 for conversion to **FF-2**; NRAB Opa Locka 10.08.36; NRAB Glenview 11.05.37. Wrecked on 04.09.38 at 1125 at Wright Field (OH). Damaged beyond repair :

![The first FF-1 to be assigned to the VF-5B was BuNo 9351, which is seen at the factory, with freshly painted codes 5-F-1 for the Squadron's leader. But the cwoling has yet to be painted.]

The first FF-1 to be assigned to the VF-5B was BuNo 9351, which is seen at the factory, with freshly painted codes 5-F-1 for the Squadron's leader. But the cwoling has yet to be painted. *(National Archives)*

The same BuNo 9351 some time later. The name of its pilot is now written under the cokpit and the cowling has also received its red paint. *(National Archives)*

"The pilot landed at Wright Field, Dayton (OH), with the wheels in a retracted position."
[Lt (jg) J.W.Hurley, USNR, with 1,456.4 hours flying time including 31.0 on type in the last three months, safe]. **Str.31.10.38.** (TT: 925.8 H).

9352

(c/n 106) Del 08.06.33 Anacostia; San Diego BatFor 21.06.33 for VF-5B; San Diego BatFor for OH 29.03.34 completed 20.07.34; Norfolk BatFor 04.09.34 for VF-5B; San Diego BatFor for OH 18.06.35 completed 15.11.35; NAF 20.04.36 for **FF-2** conversion completed 03.07.36; NRAB Opa Locka 13.07.36; NRAB Glenview 01.06.37; NAS Norfolk 31.10.40 for OH completed 10.04.41; NRAB Glenview 04.03.42. **Str. 09.04.42.**

9353

(c/n 107) Del 08.06.33 Anacostia; San Diego BatFor 21.06.33 for VF-5B; San Diego BatFor for OH 29.03.34 completed 03.08.34; Norfolk BatFor 31.08.34; VF-5B 31.08.34; San Diego BatFor 29.07.35 for OH completed 10.11.35; NAF 20.04.36 for conversion to **FF-2** completed 08.07.36; NRAB Grosse Isle 13.07.36; NAS Anacostia 01.11.40; INA Grumman 08.11.40; NAF 31.01.41. **Str.31.10.41.** Became a ground instructional airframe at Norfolk Aviation Mechanical School.

9354

(c/n 108) Del 29.06.33 San Diego BatFor for VF-5B; Norfolk BatFor 21.08.34; San Diego BatFor 27.08.34 for OH completed 02.11.34; VF-5B 15.11.34; San Diego BatFor 18.11.35; NAF 29.11.35 for **FF-2** conversion, completed 24.02.36; NRAB Grosse Isle 09.03.36. **Str. 30.11.38** after its overhaul was not authorized due to the cost. (TT: 1,138.2 H).

FF-1 BuNo 9354 warming-up for another training flight. It was first coded 5-F-4, but this was changed to 5-F-9 after its overhaul in November 1934. *(National Archives)*

U.S. NAVY

FF-2

9353

3

Grumman FF-2 BuNo 9353, NRAB Grosse Isle, 1937.

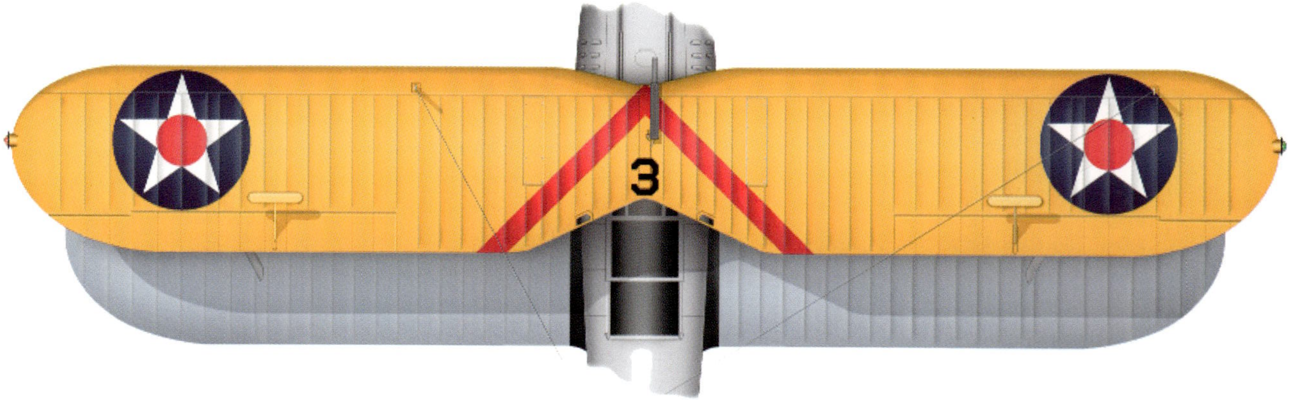

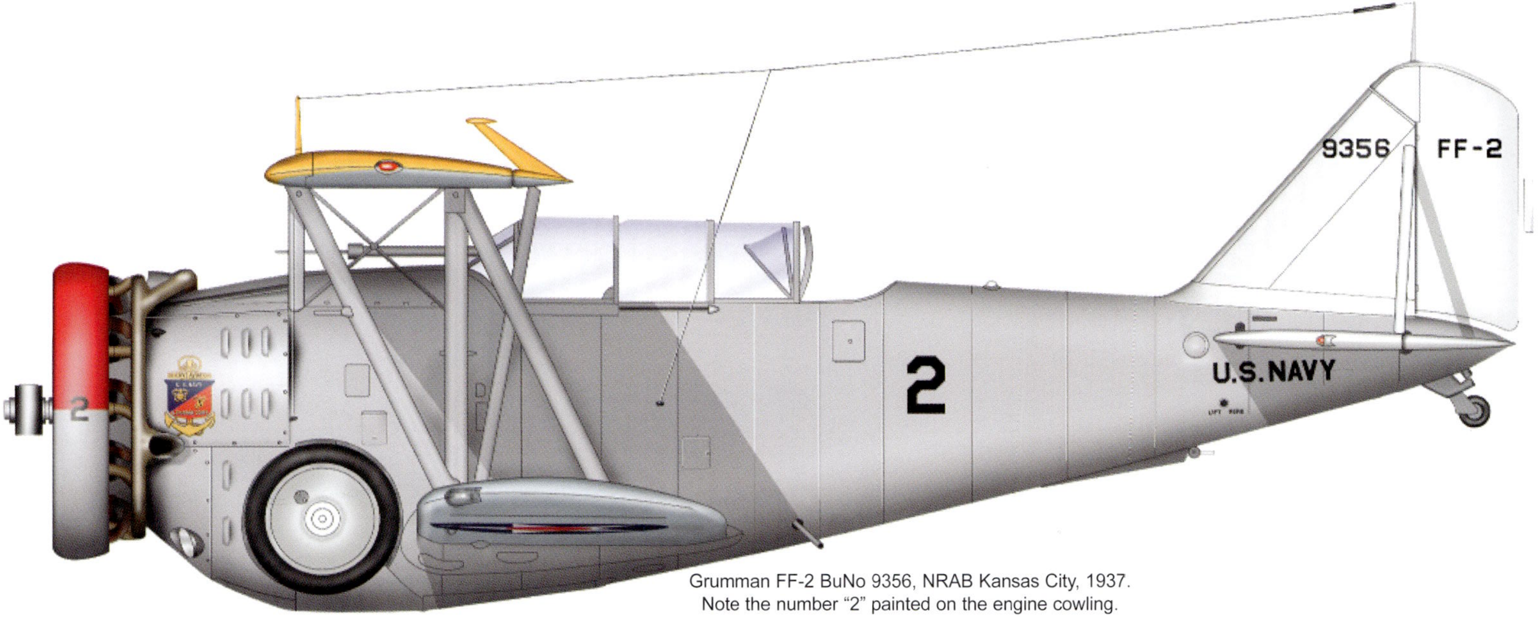

Grumman FF-2 BuNo 9356, NRAB Kansas City, 1937.
Note the number "2" painted on the engine cowling.

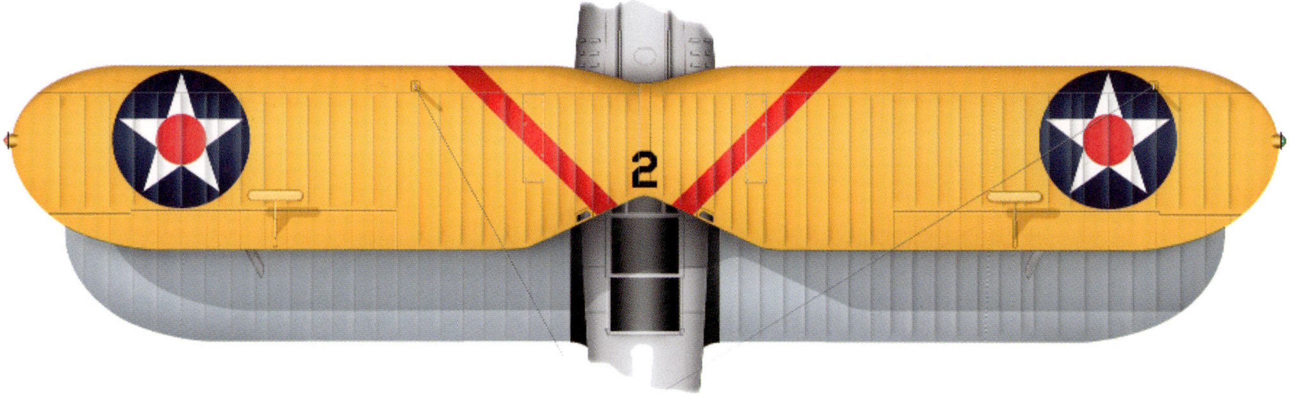

9355

(c/n 109) Del 29.06.33 San Diego BatFor for VF-5B; San Diego BatFor 06.02.35 for OH completed 03.04.35; NAF 11.02.35; San Diego BatFor 22.04.35; VF-5B 23.04.35; San Diego BatFor 21.06.35; VF-5B 31.07.35; San Diego BatFor 15.04.36; NAF 22.05.36 for **FF-2** conversion completed 13.08.36; NRAB Kansas 21.08.36; NRAB Minneapolis 21.10.39; NAS Jacksonville (Aviation Mechanical School) 29.05.41. **Str.30.06.41.** (TT: 1,168.6 H)

9356

(c/n 110) Del 29.06.33 San Diego BatFor for VF-5B; San Diego BatFor 29.03.34 for OH completed 27.07.34; Norfolk BatFor 02.09.34; VF-5B 05.09.34; San Diego BatFor 01.11.35; NAF 21.11.35 for **FF-2** conversion completed 22.04.36; NRAB Kansas 01.03.36, NAS Anacostia 20.10.40; BAD-1 Quantico 01.11.40; Air Detachment Parks Island 27.03.41; NAS Jacksonville (Aviation Mechanical School) 06.11.41. **Str.29.11.41.**

After its conversion to FF-2, BuNo 9356 served at the NRAB Kansas City as #2. The tail and stabilisers are white. *(National Archives)*

9357

(c/n 111) Del 29.06.33 San Diego BatFor for VF-5B; Norfolk BatFor 21.08.34; San Diego BatFor 27.08.34 for OH completed 01.12.34; VF-5B 03.12.34; San Diego BatFor 08.04.36; NAF 01.05.36 for **FF-2** conversion completed 28.07.36; NRAB St Louis 04.08.36; Gina Wright Field (Dayton) 31.10.40; NAF 28.05.41; Gina Wright Field 28.06.41; NRAB Glenview date unrecorded; Damaged beyond repair on 04.07.42, Bear Ford Wayne, (IN) at 19.00.

"The pilot was forced to land in a grass field due to the probable failure of the master rod bearing caused by a lack of lubricating oil. Investigation of oil consumption on previous flights showed the this should be less than 1 gallon per hour. The pilot reported no evidence of oil leaks and no indication of an excessive of consumption of oil during the flight prior to being forced to land. The pilot also reported that after landing, less than a quart of oil was drained from oil tank and pump. Since the oil tank could hold 8.5 gallons of oil, and plane had flown less than 3 hours since leaving Wright Field, where it was last landed, it appears that the accident resulted from the failure of the ground crew to properly refill the oil tank."

[Cdmr B.J.Connell, USN, with 3,662.4 hours flying time including 15.0 on type in the last three months, safe]. **Str.31.07.42.**

BuNo 9358 warming up while serving with VF-5B. As aircraft #8, the upper part of the cowling should have been painted blue, but it is not the case here, and the cowling may be a new unpainted one. *(National Archives)*

The same FF-1 BuNo 9358 photographed after its first overhaul and now flying as 5-F-17. *(National Archives)*

A nice side view of BuNo 9359 of VF-5B. Note the name of its pilot under the cockpit. *(National Archives)*

FF-1 BuNo 9361/5-F-11 of the VF-5B is warming up for another training flight. As #11, the colour on the cowling is black. *(National Archives)*

FF-1 BuNo 9362/5-F-12 of the VF-5B. As with #11 above it belongs to the fourth (Black) section. *(National Archives)*

BuNo 9362 after being converted to an FF-2. Note the rudder stripes of the reserve aircraft, but the FF-2s were rarely painted like this. *(National Archives)*

9358

(c/n 112) Del 10.07.33 San Diego BatFor for VF-5B; Norfolk BatFor 21.08.34; San Diego BatFor 27.08.34 for OH completed 23.11.34; VF-5B 26.11.34; San Diego BatFor 18.11.35; NAF 02.12.35 for **FF-2** conversion completed 16.03.36; NRAB St Louis 22.03.36; NAF (Instructional Section) 21.10.40. **Str.31.05.41.** Became a ground instructional airframe at Jacksonville Aviation Mechanical School.

9359

(c/n 113) Del 10.07.33 San Diego BatFor for VF-5B; San Diego BatFor 21.11.34 for OH completed 08.02.35; VF-5B 01.03.35; San Diego BatFor 15.04.36; NAF 28.05.36 for **FF-2** conversion completed 25.08.36; NRAB Grosse Isle 28.08.36; NAS Anacostia 01.11.40; NAS Lake Hurst 04.11.40. **Str.29.11.40**. Became a ground instructional airframe at Norfolk Aviation Mechanical School.

9360

(c/n 114) Del 03.08.33 San Diego BatFor; VF-5B 04.08.33; Norfolk BatFor 21.08.34; San Diego BatFor 27.08.34 for OH completed 09.11.34; VF-5B 15.11.34; San Diego BatFor 08.04.36 for OH; Crashed on 24.04.36 1.4 miles N.W. of Clover Field (Santa Monica, CA); San Diego 28.04.36.

"This aircraft was one of a flight of two planes on an extended flight from NAS San Diego (CA) to Clover Field (Santa Monica, CA). Prior to approaching for a landing at Santa Monica the pilot of this plane became separated from the other plane and was evidently making a right turn over Rustic Canyon, in the foothills of Santa Monica mountains, 1.4 miles northwest of Clover Field. The aircraft and engine were apparently functioning normally. The plane was evidently nose down in a rather tight right turn at high speed with the wheels retracted. The plane struck the hill on the east side of the canyon, about ten feet from the crest, in full flight with the propeller and bomb racks apparently striking first and the engine and fuselage immediately thereafter. Fire started immediately and the plane rolled down the hill. The plane was almost completely demolished, and burned, with fragments of wreckage scattered over an area about 100 feet by 150 feet."

[Lt (jg) A.D.J.Farrell, USN, with 1,260.0 hours flying time and ACM1c W.V. Kerr, USN, both killed]. **Str.29.05.36.** (TT: 636.3 H).

9361

(c/n 115) Del 03.08.33 San Diego BatFor; VF-5B 04.08.33 ; San Diego BatFor 16.11.34. Wrecked on 02.02.35 at 0850:

"Crashed on bad weather during a ferry flight between NAS San Diego and Naval Aircraft Factory, 23 miles east of Millsap, Texas."

[Lt (jg) C.W.Pate, USN (from VS-1), with 1,339.6 hours flying time including 79.1 on type in the last three months and Lt (jg) S.G.Burgess (from VF-3), USN, both killed]. **Str.31.08.35.**

9362

(c/n 116) Del 03.08.33 San Diego BatFor; VF-5B 04.08.33; Norfolk BatFor 04.09.34 for OH completed 11.09.34; San Diego BatFor 22.10.35; NAF 21.11.35 for **FF-2** conversion completed 03.03.36; NRAB Philadelphia (VN-5RD4) 03.03.36; NRAB Glenview 01.07.37; NAS Norfolk 31.10.40; Norfolk 29.05.41 for OH completed 25.07.41; NRAB Glenview 02.03.42. **Str.30.04.42.**

9363

(c/n 117) Del 10.08.33 San Diego BatFor; NAF 10.08.33; San Diego BatFor 27.10.33; VF-5B 29.10.33; NAF 17.08.34 for OH completed 16.11.34; San Diego BatFor 14.01.35; VF-5B

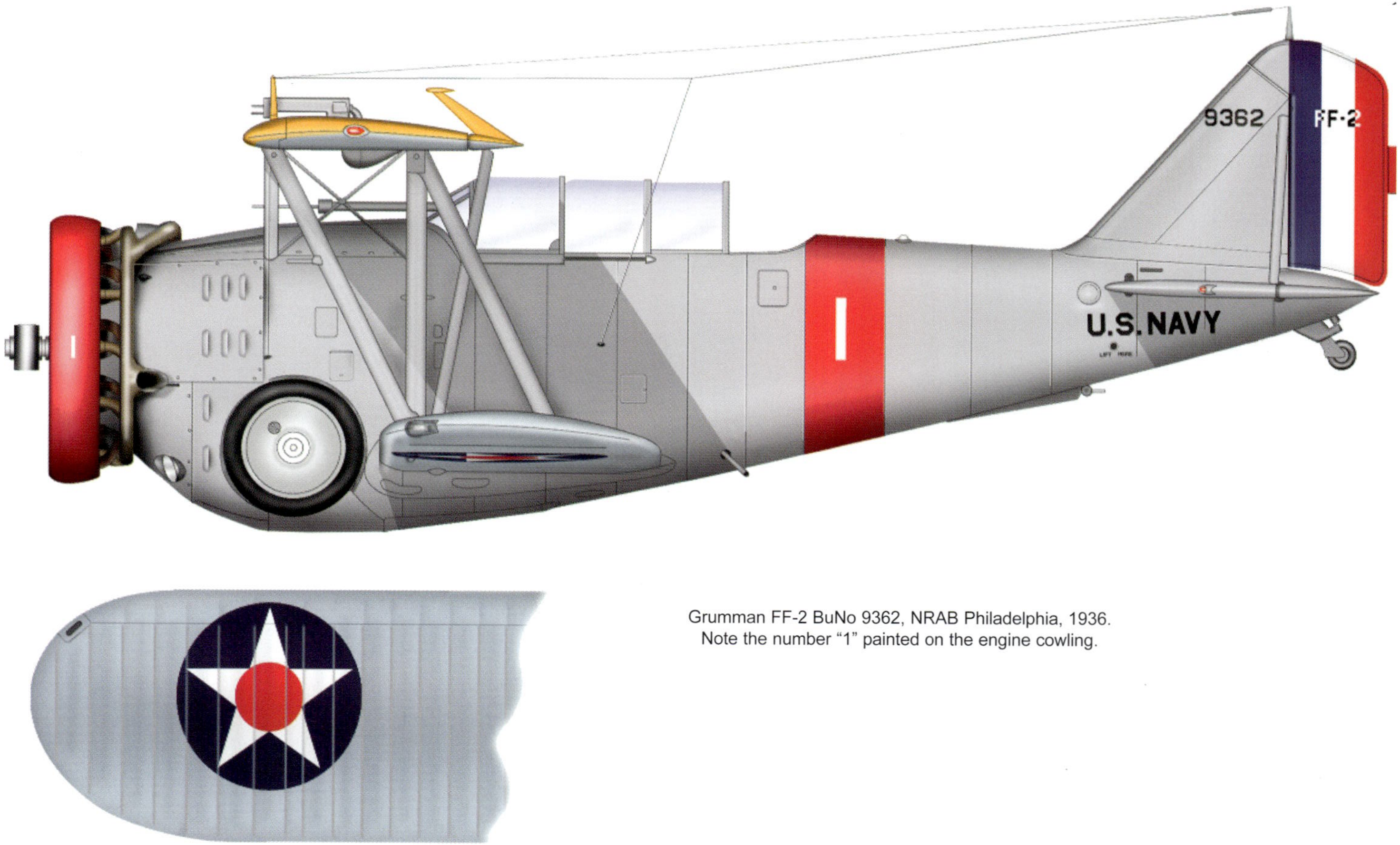

Grumman FF-2 BuNo 9362, NRAB Philadelphia, 1936.
Note the number "1" painted on the engine cowling.

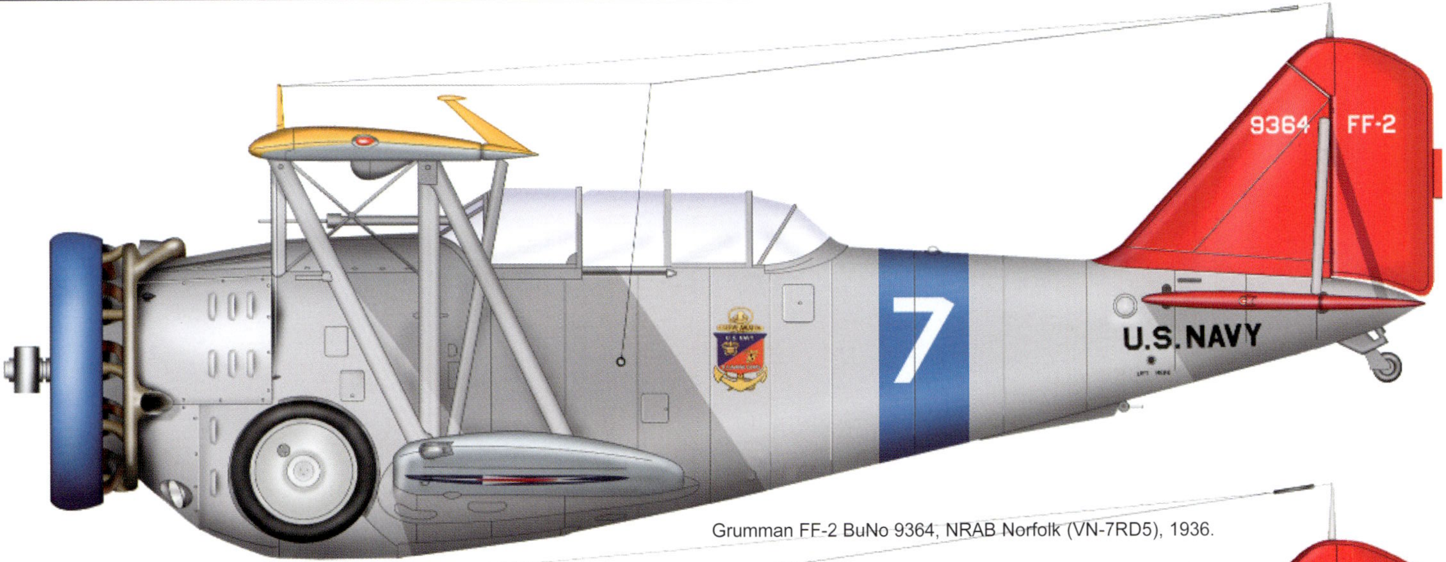

Grumman FF-2 BuNo 9364. NRAB Norfolk (VN-7RD5), 1936.

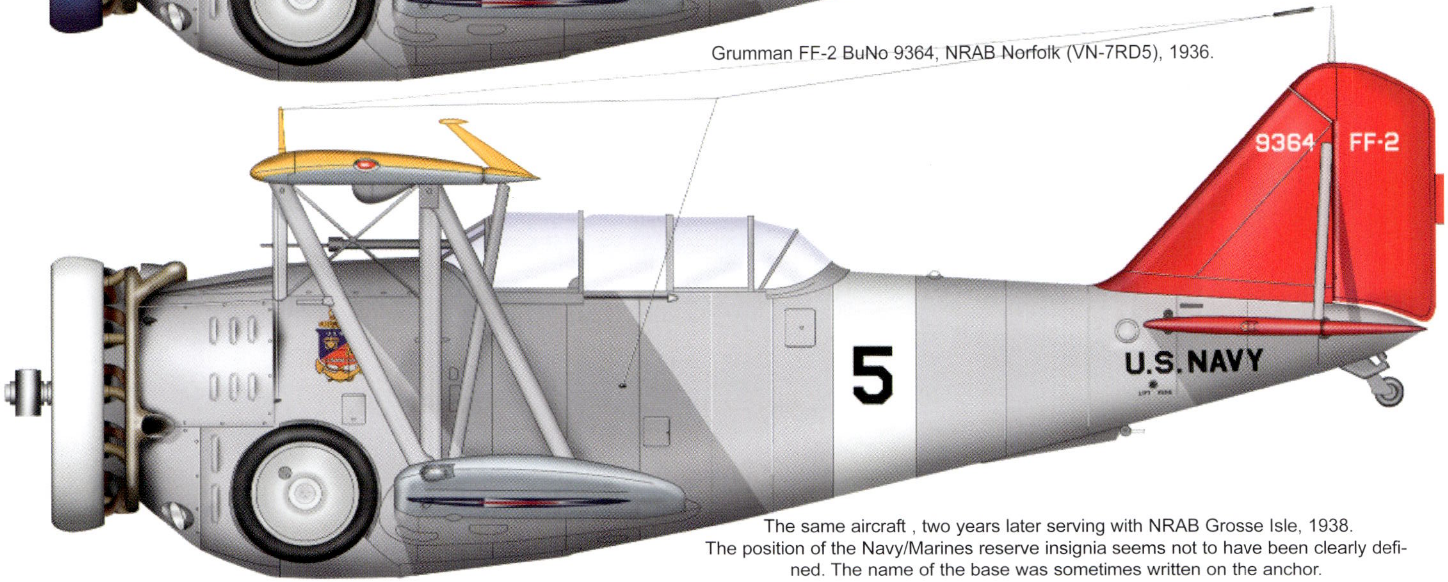

The same aircraft, two years later serving with NRAB Grosse Isle, 1938. The position of the Navy/Marines reserve insignia seems not to have been clearly defined. The name of the base was sometimes written on the anchor.

16.01.35; San Diego BatFor 22.10.35; NAF 12.12.35 for **FF-2** conversion completed 05.03.36; NRAB Opa Locka 19.03.36; NRAB Great Lakes 01.06.37; Crashed on 10.07.37 at 1538 at Glenview: "Accident was caused by the failure of the pilot to recover from an apparent flat spin. Aircraft landed in such an attitude that caused the aircraft to stop at the place of contact. The aircraft's final position was horizontal. Aircraft deficiency in the upward travel of the elevators. Stops are set 3/16" closer than on some of the other FF-2s at this Station. This deficiency is approximately 6-1/2°, at 3 miles NE of Glenview field."

[Lt. E.L.Johansen, USNR, with 3,210.1 hours flying time including 32.0 on type in the last three months, killed and AMM1c R.J.Hedien, USNR, injured]. **Str.31.08.37** (TT: 817.2)

Leader of the third (Blue) section was flying this FF-2 BuNo 9364 with a blue cowling and fuselage band. The tail is believed to be red. Note the Reserve insignia which was painted under the gunner's seat. The location of the insignia varied from one aircraft from to another. (National Archives)

9364

(c/n 118) Del 10.08.33 NAF 10.08.33; San Diego BatFor 02.10.33; VF-5B 26.10.33; San Diego BatFor 24.04.35; Norfolk BatFor 08.05.35; NAF for OH 05.06.35 completed 19.08.35; San Diego BatFor 03.09.35; NAF for conversion to **FF-2** 13.12.35, completed 14.04.36; VN-7RD5 Norfolk 20.04.36; NRAB Grosse Isle 01.10.36; NAS Anacostia 01.11.40; INA New York 06.11.40. **Str.21.01.42** as obsolete. Became a ground instructional airframe at Chicago (Glenview) Aviation Mechanical School.

9365

(c/n 119) Del 10.08.33 NAF 10.08.33; San Diego BatFor 23.08.33; VF-5B 29.08.33; San Diego BatFor 15.11.34; NAF 05.02.35 for OH completed 01.04.35; San Diego BatFor 22.04.35; VF-5B 23.04.35; San Diego BatFor 14.04.36; NAF for conversion to **FF-2** 14.05.36, completed 31.07.36; VN-5RD4/NAF 04.08.36; NAF 07.08.37; NRAB Minneapolis 30.10.37. Crashed on 24.09.38 at base at 1400 :
"The accident occurred on a normal take-off on a scheduled flight for training purposes. The pilot taxied from the ramp at the NRAB hangar to the northwest corner of the field. The take-off was

to the southwest. After gaining considerable speed, the airplane hit a small bump, which lifted it a few inches from the ground. Flying speed was not sufficient to hold it off, and on returning to the ground the left wheel gave way, followed almost immediately by the right wheel, causing the fuselage to settle at which time the left wing tip dug in slightly and the aircraft assumed nearly a vertical position before dropping back to upright position. It was noticed immediately after the accident that the red warning light was on. A very careful inspection of the landing gear mechanism was made by the board and no defect in material or operation was discovered. After the accident the wheels were retracted.

From the statement of the pilot to the board the red warning light was not on during warmup, taxying, or start of the take-off, that the release handle was in "locked" position, and the fact that the landing gear mechanism was in perfect working order after the accident, the only conclusion that can be drawn is that the release handle was in some way changed to "release" during the take-off run."

[Col. M.J. Maas, USMCR, with 1,100.0 hours flying time including 8.0 on type in the last three months, slightly injured]. **Str. 31.10.38.** (TT: 967.3)

9366

(c/n 120) Del 07.09.33 NAF; San Diego BatFor 02.11.33; VF-1B 02.03.34; VF-5B 03.03.34; San Diego BatFor 15.08.35; NAF 21.08.35 for conversion to **FF-2** completed 07.02.36; NRAB Miami 19.02.36; NRAB Glenview 01.06.37; Crashed 08.08.38 at 1130 at Glenview.

"The accident was caused by a stall at low altitude while approaching the field for landing. The contributory cause of the stall was not known as the pilot had no recollection of events prior to the accident due to injuries received. It was the opinion of the Board, based on testimony of eye-witnesses, that pilot allowed plane's speed to fall below safe gliding speed during approach, and that a too rapid forward movement of the throttle prevented engine response to time to avoid the complete loss of flying speed." Damaged beyond repair.

[Lt G.G.Lamb, USNR, with 940.1 hours flying time including 9.0 on type in the last three months, and A-S/O-2 A.R.Erickson, USNR, both slightly injured]. **Str.30.09.38** (TT: 953.5).

BuNo 9367 was one the 18 FF-1s assigned to VF-5B when the type was introduced into service. It was later converted to an FF-2. *(National Archives)*

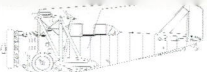

9367

(c/n 121) Del 07.09.33 NAF; San Diego BatFor 27.10.33; VF-5B 29.10.33; San Diego BatFor 08.01.35; VF-5B 16.08.35; San Diego BatFor 15.04.35 for OH completed 17.05.35; NAF 20.05.36 for conversion to **FF-2** completed 18.08.36; NRAB Kansas City 25.08.36; Anacostia 20.10.40; BAD-1 Quantico 25.10.40; Crashed during a ferry flight, 08.07.42, Cedar Point (MD), at 1120. "From the best information available it appears that the underlying cause of the accident was the failure of the pilot to give the plane the gun soon enough, after finding that he had overshot the landing field, to enable him to clear the obstacles at the end of the field. It was necessary for the pilot to pull up sharply to clear these obstacles with the result that he squashed into the tree tops." Damaged beyond repair.
[TSgt H.F.Heyliger, USMCR, with 309.1 hours flying time safe]. **Str.31.07.42.**

9368

(c/n 122) Del 07.09.33 NAF; Anacostia 17.01.34; San Diego BatFor 24.01.34 and allocated to VF-5B the same day; San Diego BatFor 13.11.34 for OH completed 25.01.35; VF-5B 01.03.35; San Diego BatFor 08.04.36; NAF 01.05.36 for conversion to **FF-2** completed 23.07.36; NRAB Kansas City 04.08.36. **Str.31.05.39.** (TT: 921.9)

9369

(c/n 123) Del 22.09.33 NAF; Anacostia 17.01.34; San Diego BatFor 24.01.34; VF-5B 24.01.34; San Diego BatFor 08.08.35; NAF 21.08.35 for conversion to **FF-2** completed 12.02.36; NRAB Minneapolis 23.02.36. **Str.31.03.41** as obsolete. (TT: 1,127.2). Became a ground instructional airframe at Norfolk Aviation Mechanical School.

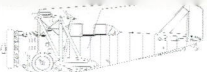

BuNo 9369 was stored at first before being issued to VF-5B, in January 1934, as replacement aircraft. *(National Archives)*

As with many other FF-1s, BuNo 9369 was converted to an FF-2 and served as such at NRAB Minneapolis. The Reserve insignia is now located just behind the cowling ring. *(National Archives)*

9370

(c/n 124) Del 22.09.33 NAF; Anacostia 13.02.34; San Diego BatFor date unrecorded; VF-5B 10.03.34; Norfolk BatFor 03.07.34; VF-5B 16.07.34; Norfolk BatFor 31.08.34 for OH completed 11.07.35; San Diego BatFor 19.07.35; VF-5B 12.08.35; San Diego 14.04.36; NAF 28.05.36 for conversion to *FF-2* completed 23.09.36; NRAB Kansas 28.09.36. Crashed on 08.01.38 at Kansas City (KS) at 1500 :

"Captain Southworth took off from Fairfax Airport and proceeded to the gunnery range which lies approximately 5 miles north of Kansas City (KS) and runs east to west. When 6,000 feet altitude was reached the two planes commenced their gunnery practice. Due to northwest winds and poor visibility the planes unknowingly drifted over Kansas City, Kansas. Captain Southworth placed his plane in a stalled turn to the left to gain a more advantageous position. In recovering from the stalled turn position he applied right rudder and forward stick. The airplane went into a left spin with nose about 30°. All efforts to recover from the spin were unavailing. The controls were ineffective and power from engine increased the spin. When the plane reached approximately 2,000 feet altitude Captain Southworth gave the order to jump and the airplane. Private Gregory jumped soon after. The plane crashed into the side of a house at 1121 Stewart Avenue, Kansas City (KS)."
[Capt. B.B.Southworth, USMCR, with 1,162.0 hours flying time including 5.0 on type in the last three months, safe and Pvt W.H.Gregory, USMCR slightly injured]. **Str.31.01.38** (TT: 575.9 H).

9371

(c/n 125) 22.09.33 San Diego BatFor; NAF 21.12.33; Norfolk/Anacostia 09.01.34; San Diego for VB-5B 24.01.34; San Diego BatFor 24.04.35; Norfolk BatFor 08.05.35; NAF 05.06.35 for OH completed 19.08.35; San Diego BatFor 03.09.35; NAF 13.12.35 for conversion to *FF-2* completed 10.04.36; VN-5ND4/NAF 15.04.36; NAF 05.09.36 for OH completed 09.04.37; VN-5RD4 Phildelphia 07.05.37; NRAB Glenview 29.06.37; NAS Norfolk 31.10.40; NRAB Glenview 02.03.42 **Str.30.04.42**.

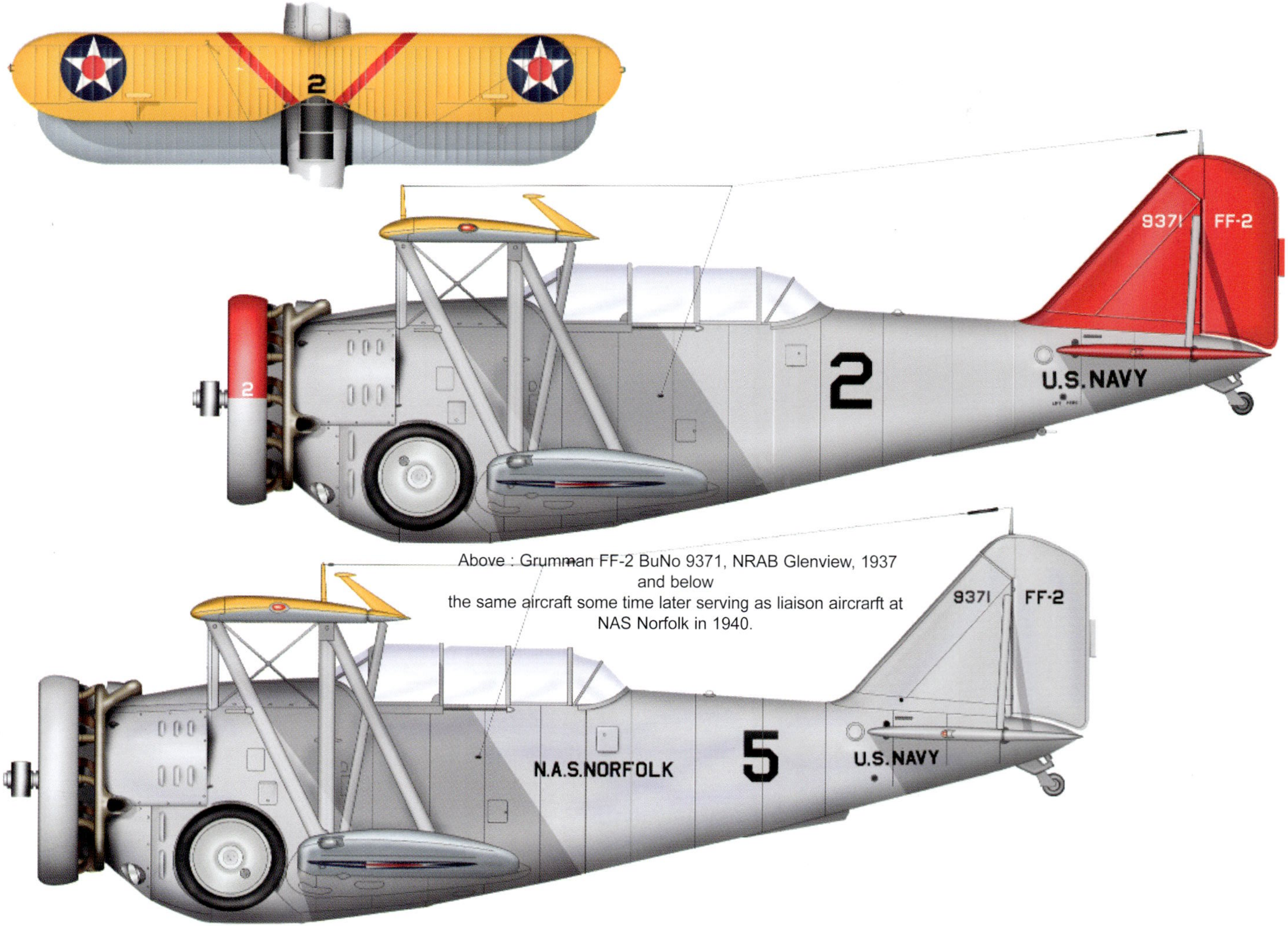

FF-2

9371

U.S. NAVY

2

FF-2

9371

U.S. NAVY

5

N.A.S. NORFOLK

2

Above : Grumman FF-2 BuNo 9371, NRAB Glenview, 1937 and below the same aircraft some time later serving as liaison aircrarft at NAS Norfolk in 1940.

FF-2 BuNo 9371 believed to have belonged to NRAB Glenview in 1937. There is no Reserve insignia painted on this aircraft. At the end of its career, BuNo 9371 served as liaison aircraft # 5 for NAS Norfolk, thence the inscription "NAS NORFOLK" painted on the fuselage. The aircraft was left in natural metal finish. *(National Archives)*

9372

(c/n 126) Del 10.10.33 NAF; San Diego BatFor 08.02.34; VF-5B 16.03.34; NAF 07.06.34 for OH completed 30.08.34; VF-5B 04.09.34; San Diego BatFor 22.10.35; NAF 16.12.35 for conversion to **FF-2**, completed 10.03.36; NRAB Minneapolis (VS-10R) 24.03.36. Crashed on 04.08.38 at Camp Ripley landing Field (MN) at 1205 :

"The plane was coming in for landing when ground crew noticed wheels were still retracted, Attempts were made to attract pilot's attention without success. Plane was in normal landing condition and coming in about 60 knots. Plane slid on belly for 60 feet and then went over on nose, landing on its back 7 feet from point of burying its nose. Conditions of the field was

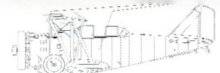

dry but sandy. The warning light was still showing after the crash."
[Lt C.F.Luethi, USNR, with 850.0 hours flying time including 23.1 on type in the last three months and AS-O2 D.H.Ledin, USNR both safe]. **Str.31.08.38.** (TT: 851.2 H).

9373

(c/n 127) 10.10.33 NAF; San Diego BatFor 13.02.34; VF-5B 16.03.34; San Diego BatFor 13.09.35; NAF 24.09.35 for conversion to **FF-2** completed 14.02.36; NRAB St Louis 20.02.36. **Str.30.09.40** as OH not authorized, having reached its operating limit. (TT:1,818.3) NAS Jacksonville to Trade Schools 28.10.40.

9374

(c/n 128) Del 10.10.33 NAF; San Diego BatFor 13.02.34; Norfolk BatFor 04.09.34 for VF5B; San Diego BatFor 01.11.35; NAF 17.12.35 for conversion to **FF-2** completed 31.03.36; NRAB Grosse Ile 03.04.36; Crashed 18.07.36 at Murfreesboro (TN) at 1139. **Str.31.08.36.** (TT: 434.6).
"There were no eye witnesses to the crash. Pilot and passenger were returning from an authorised cross country flight to Pensacola (FL). They landed at Sky Harbor Airport, Murfreesboro (TN) and took on a full load of gas. With a storm approaching from the northwest the pilot took off with the apparent intention of circumnavigating it to the north or northwest which also was on his course to Nashville or Luisville, the normal course en route to Gross Ile. When last seen, however, he was on a southerly course crossing the airport at an altitude of about 5,000 feet. From a pocket watch belonging at ACMM Yassay the crash apparently occurred at 11.39 C.S.T. at which time the watch had stopped. The location was on a farm about 5 miles north to northeast of the field and during a violent thunder and lightning storm. From all appearances the plane struck the ground at high speed on its right side, wing tips first, cartwheeled and becoming completely demolished. The plane and equipment were partially burned, the flames being extinguished by the intense rain. It could not be definitely determined whether the fire began in the air or after contact with the ground. The plane was equipped with radio and had an aerial from the wing tip to the vertical stabiliser."
[Ens. O.W.Lowmaster, USNR, with 898.7 hours flying time including 11.2 on type in the last three months, and ACMM A.J.Yassay, USNR, both killed]. **Str.31.08.36**. (TT: 434.6 H).

9375

(c/n 129) Del 01.11.33 NAF; San Diego BatFor 08.02.34; Norfolk BatFor 31.08.34; VB-5B 31.08.34; San Diego BatFor 21.10.35; NAF 17.12.35 for conversion to **FF-2** completed 19.03.36; NRAB Kansas City 28.03.36; NAS Anacostia 25.10.40; INA Wright Paterson 06.11.40; NAF Oper. 18.12.40; **Str.23.01.42.** Became ground instructional airframe at Chicago (Glenview) 07.02.42.

9376

(c/n 130) Del 01.11.33 NAF ; San Diego BatFor 08.02.34; VF-1B 08.02.34; San Diego BatFor 26.03.34; Norfolk BatFor 06.09.34 for VF-5B; San Diego BatFor 23.08.35 for OH completed 10.12.35; NAF 20.04.36 for conversion to **FF-2** completed 24.07.36; NRAB Minneapolis 31.07.36. NAS Jacksonville 03.06.41 for disposal. **Str.30.06.41** (TT: 989.0).

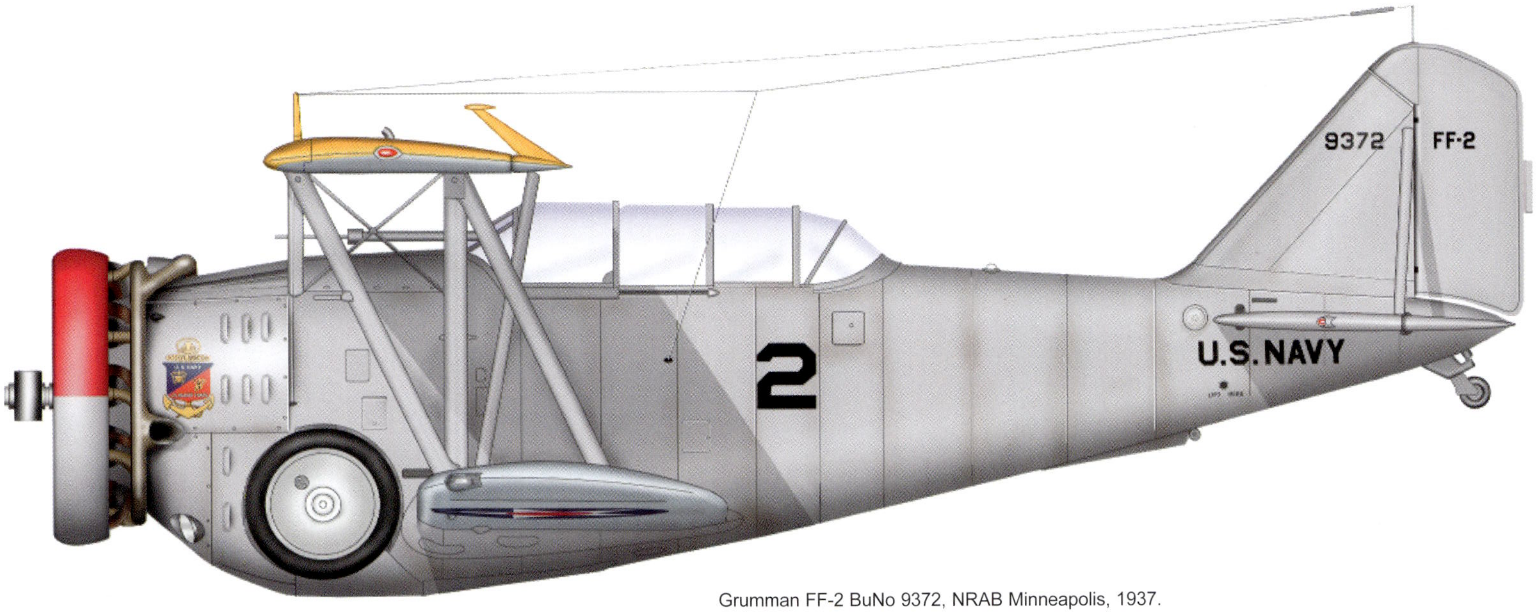

Grumman FF-2 BuNo 9372, NRAB Minneapolis, 1937.

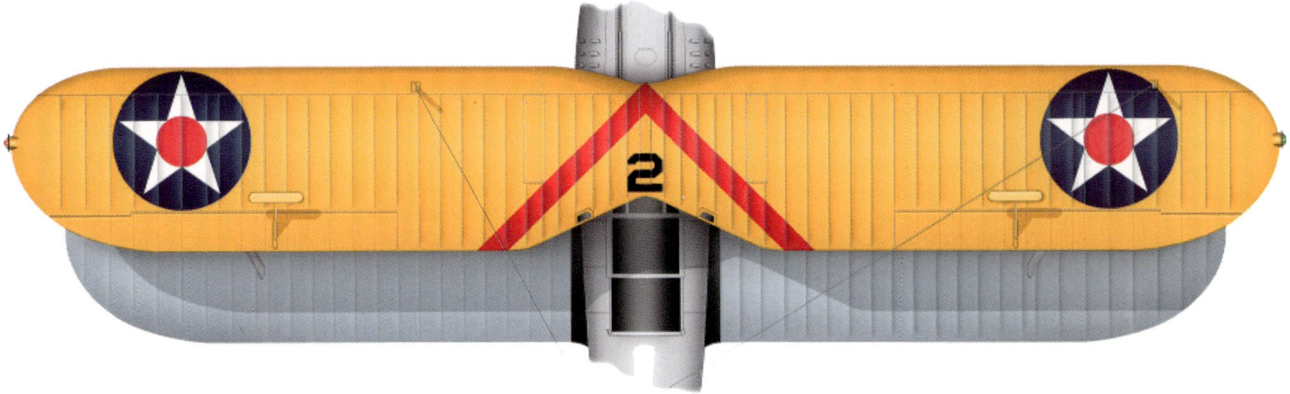

U.S. NAVY

FF-2

9372

2

THE FF IN DETAIL

Engine cowling of a FF-1 (above) and of a FF-2 (below).

The canopy in open position.

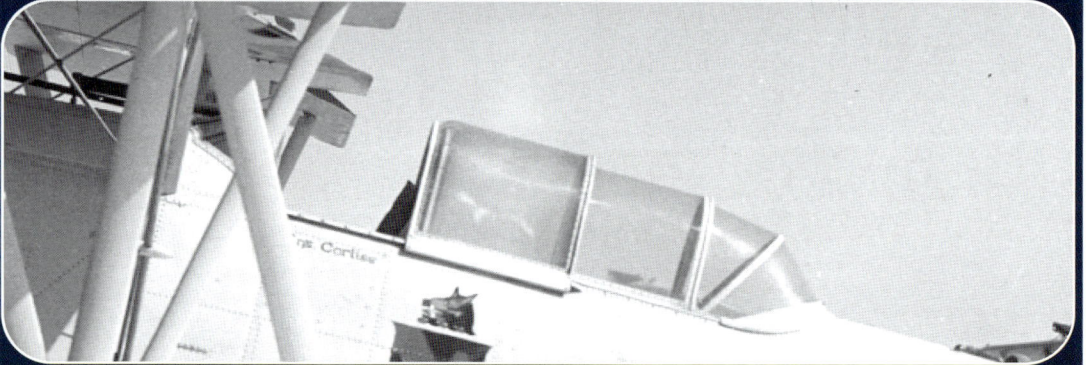

Above : the main landing gear in extended position.
Below (left) ; the emergency flotation bag panel and the telescopic gunsight (right)

The gunner's seat (above) and the rear machine-gun (below).

Rear view *(National Archives)*

VF-5B Section Colours in 1934

First Section (*Red*)

5-F-1
FF-1 BuNo 9351

5-F-2
FF-1 BuNo 9352

5-F-3
FF-1 BuNo 9353

Second Section (*White*)

5-F-4
FF-1 BuNo 9354

5-F-5
FF-1 BuNo 9355

5-F-6
FF-1 BuNo 9356

Third Section (*True Blue*)

5-F-7
FF-1 BuNo 9357

5-F-8
FF-1 BuNo 9358

5-F-9
FF-1 BuNo 9359

Fourth Section (*Black*)

5-F-10
FF-1 BuNo 9360

5-F-11
FF-1 BuNo 9361

5-F-12
FF-1 BuNo 9362

Fifth Section (*Willow Green*)

5-F-13
FF-1 BuNo 9363

5-F-14
FF-1 BuNo 9364

5-F-15
FF-1 BuNo 9365

Sixth Section (*Lemon Yellow*)

5-F-16
FF-1 BuNo 9366

5-F-17
FF-1 BuNo 9367

5-F-18
FF-1 BuNo 9368

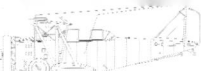

A FF-2 of an unidentified NRAB unit. Note the black "2" painted on the engine cowling. (*National Archives*).

ROLL OF HONOUR

GRUMMAN FF

Name	Rank	Origin	Date	BuNo
BURGESS, S.G.	Lt (jg)	USN	02.02.35	9361
FARRELL, A.D.J.	Lt (jg)	USN	24.04.36	9360
JOHANSEN, E.L.	Lt	USNR	10.07.37	9363
KERR, W.V.	ACM1c	USN	24.04.36	9360
LOWMASTER, O.W.	Ens.	USNR	18.07.36	9374
PATE, C.W.	Lt (jg)	USN	02.02.35	9361
YASSAY, A.J.	ACMM	USNR	18.07.36	9374

Total : 6